THE IMPOSSIBILITY OF WAR RISK INSURANCE

THE IMPOSSIBILITY OF WAR RISK INSURANCE

A paper read before the Insurance Institute of London on 15th March, 1938

by

SIR WILLIAM P. ELDERTON
C.B.E., F.I.A., F.F.A.

CAMBRIDGE
AT THE UNIVERSITY PRESS
1938

CAMBRIDGE
UNIVERSITY PRESS

University Printing House, Cambridge CB2 8BS, United Kingdom

Cambridge University Press is part of the University of Cambridge.

It furthers the University's mission by disseminating knowledge in the pursuit of education, learning and research at the highest international levels of excellence.

www.cambridge.org
Information on this title: www.cambridge.org/9781316633281

© Cambridge University Press 1938

First published 1938
First paperback edition 2016

A catalogue record for this publication is available from the British Library

ISBN 978-1-316-63328-1 Paperback

THE IMPOSSIBILITY OF WAR RISK INSURANCE

DURING the past few months letters have appeared in the Press saying that people who own property in this country ought to be able to provide some form of insurance to compensate them for damage that may be done to their property as the result of enemy action by air or by bombardment, and the letters have generally started by giving the impression that until recently this risk had been met by existing insurances. This impression is incorrect. The insurance companies never intended to cover this risk in any form, and the only changes they have made were designed to make this abundantly clear to everyone concerned. It is true to say that, generally speaking, insurances effected with Companies have excluded the risk, and the only way the risk could be covered was to a limited extent with Lloyd's. There is little doubt, moreover, that a very small proportion of the property in the United Kingdom has been insured in this way, and the property owners have not, therefore, in practice suddenly been deprived of such insurance. Even, however, if there had been a change there might have been a good reason for it, and I shall try to explain why war risk cannot properly be covered, and that any attempt to do so in advance of war will only create an illusion of security and not security itself.

It has been suggested by property owners that the risk might be covered by some sort of insurance, by a mutual pooling scheme or by a Government scheme. I propose to deal with these suggestions in that order.

The first principle in any scheme of insurance is that it must be possible to make, in advance, an estimate of a premium which would be sufficient to meet the risk it is required to cover, and, in order that this may be done, some idea must be formed of the amount of damage that will occur and of the chance of a particular property suffering; it is also necessary that the insurer can meet the liability whenever it may arise. In the case of fire insurance, long experience has shown that premiums can be fixed accurately and that the rate of loss compared with premiums remains reasonably constant year by year in this country; the insurer can therefore pay the claims. Any fluctuation in excess of the normal claims has been shown to be relatively small and could easily be met out of the accumulated reserves which insurers have put by as a safety margin for the benefit of everybody concerned. There have, in the past, been exceptional losses—such as that at San Francisco—and every prudent insurance company keeps substantial reserves in case such a loss should occur.

The first thing we must do, then, in considering the problem of insuring war risk is to see if we can calculate a premium.

The Great War gave some indication of the sort of damage that could be done in modern conditions by aircraft in this country and by bombardment and aircraft in Belgium and Northern France, but conditions have changed greatly since then, and there is little doubt that hostile aircraft can now do more damage than was done in that war because of the increase in the number and speed of planes, increased experience in flying, greater power of explosive bombs and better construction of machines. These changed conditions imply a greater range of activity and, whereas London was accessible in 1918, the Midlands and the North or West of England, and even Scotland, would be open to attack now. The present Japanese war in China has given a more modern instance of the damage that might be done to property within a short time. According to one article,* 5255 factories were destroyed in Shanghai and the damage was estimated by the Bureau of Social Affairs of the City Government of Greater Shanghai at a figure equivalent to over £40,000,000. However much we may hope that this may be an exaggerated estimate, we must, I think, conclude that the damage there and elsewhere in China is tremendous.

The difficulty in assessing a premium lies—first, in the impossibility of making any accurate estimate of the damage to property in this country that may result in the event of war. We must always bear in mind, in any risk to property, that the damage must be related to the density with which a country is populated, for it is clear that bombardment or aircraft would cause far greater damage in a crowded city than in wide open spaces with scattered villages, and secondly, even if we could make such an estimate, in ascertaining in advance when the damage is likely to occur, for war may start this year or there may be no war for ten or twenty years to come. The uncertainty when war may start can be exemplified by the recent Japanese invasion of China when there was no declaration of war, and it is true to say that neither property owners nor insurers in China foresaw it, with any degree of certainty, a couple of months before.

It can be argued that if the power to attack has become intensified, there must also be an improvement in defence, but no one can pretend that the defence in aerial warfare will prevent extensive damage to the cities of both combatants. Improved defence against improved attack might merely give a better chance to defend towns in one part

* From *Oriental Affairs*, Dec. 1937.

of England than in another—the greater speed of fighting planes might mean that we should not have time to get a defence force of planes up in time to defend London, Maidstone, or coastal towns against a raid, but would have a fair chance of doing so before Birmingham, Bristol or Edinburgh were attacked. But whatever views individuals may hold on such a point or on possible other methods of defence, we cannot estimate the extent of the damage that might be done to any town.

I shall now assume for a moment that a few insurers think that an estimate of the risk can be made and decide that the annual premium to be charged is one shilling per cent of the value of the property, and, for the sake of argument, I shall assume that that rate is correct, and that it is the net premium receivable after all expenses of collection, etc. have been met.

This means that the damage done to the properties insured will, on the average, over the number of years during which the premium is received be £500 for every £1,000,000 insured; but if the premium mentioned were correct it took into account the frequency of war, and averaged the premium over the years without war as well as over those with war. If, for instance, war comes once in twenty years, the damage when it does occur is twenty times as great as that assumed in the year's premium, and the claims in war would not be £500 but £10,000 for each £1,000,000 insured. Now even assuming the rate of premium quoted is correct, it is clear from this argument that no insurer would have the money available to meet the claims from the premiums received if war occurred in the first year. It would be necessary to pay, for damage, twenty times the amount received in premiums. In other words, there would be an immediate loss of nineteen times the premium received.

The amount of fire insurances effected on property and contents in London alone is over £2,000,000,000 and on the figures given above the total damage from war is £20,000,000, and on our assumptions the premiums received would have been £1,000,000. If the one shilling per cent rate had been based on the assumption of a war every ten years the assumed total damage on properties insured against fire for London is £10,000,000. Without any feeling of panic, I should have thought that that damage might be done in less than a month! If insurance companies were to cover the risk, the difference between the £20,000,000 damage and £1,000,000 premiums would have to be found out of reserve funds in other departments of this business. The reserves set aside to make fire insurance, accident, marine and motor insurance safe—to make them real insurance—would be taken to pay these war risk claims.

There are, however, other difficulties. When a great war comes, the ordinary work of a country undergoes fundamental changes: the energies of the workers are deflected from ordinary channels into others connected with the war. Building operations, and the manufacture of furniture, for instance, are postponed and their place is taken by the manufacture of armaments. At the end of the last war building was far in arrear, not only because there was a shortage of houses and the contents for houses, but also because repairs, that in normal times would have been considered necessary, were years in arrear. This implies that when war comes we cannot replace, immediately, the damage done: labour will not be available and a Government might even prohibit rebuilding because work could be better used in the active prosecution of the war, or because rebuilding in a vulnerable area would be asking for further immediate losses. If therefore insurances were granted against war risk and the insurers could assess the damage in terms of money, the payment would not necessarily mean re-instatement.

Another difficulty will occur to anyone with memory of the last war. If an insurer tries to cover the risk and relies on reserves kept for other classes of business in order to pay the claims he is faced with, he is involved in the further difficulty that he cannot estimate what the value of those reserves will be if he has to realise them during, or even immediately after, a war. In a war, depreciation of securities occurs and investments in Government securities may fall by half their value, while if, as has happened in some European countries, currency depreciates violently the reserves may disappear as compared with the replacement value of goods insured. It may be suggested that there is a flaw in this argument because even if there is no insurance of war risks, the assets will depreciate during a war. Of course they will, but the fire and accident risks that are covered are independent of war and will not, necessarily, occur in catastrophic dimensions at the time of depreciation, whereas war risk and depreciation go together.

I cannot think that it is wise, or even fair, that a margin built up out of profits made from certain classes of insurance, and put aside for their safety, should be imperilled in order to underwrite an extremely dangerous kind of catastrophic risk not hitherto covered. The result of imperilling those reserves would be a general demand for their protection, and if they were fully protected the war risks would only be able to rely on their own funds, and this would turn the supposed war risk insurance into a mere pooling scheme of the kind that I shall discuss a little later. Moreover, many of these reserves are wanted in connection with the world-wide business of insurance and to damage them might mean the death-blow to the foreign business of British insurance companies: a business which has been built up over many years and has won the highest regard for British insurance. The laws of some countries provide that assets have to be deposited for the security of policy-holders, and the immediate withdrawal of any part of the assets hypothecated in these countries would be impossible.

Let us assume, yet once more, that some insurer covers, or pretends to cover, the risk, and that many insurances are effected when there is some immediate risk of war. The danger passes and peace is certain. The insurer keeps the premiums and has made an apparent profit. No one now asks for the insurances, but five years later there is another scare and the same thing happens again. And then, perhaps, the next time, war comes. The losses are tremendous and we are back at the old difficulties. There is not the same perpetuity of risk as in fire or motor or marine or death insurance—it is intermittent. We are reminded that people are inclined to ask for such insurances when they think there is an appreciable risk of an early war and not in times of happy and continuous peace. This is what has happened since the Great War; there was no real demand for war risk insurance until very recently and then, I think, only because people were reminded that they were not getting it: a very human attitude at which we may smile in passing.

The arguments used hitherto have given as a starting-point that it is possible to assess a premium. But if a war started to-morrow, no one can estimate whether the risk could be met by a 10s. per cent rate or a 3 per cent rate, nor can anyone know when there will be a war nor how long it will last. In other words, to pretend, first, to assess a premium and then to cover the risk would not be insurance: it is the reverse of insurance—gambling.

It may be remarked that the insurance of property on land against risks of war is different both from insuring property on the high seas against war damage and from life assurance. The marine risk is not fixed as regards place and a catastrophe among marine risks is relatively small. Moreover, the risk is limited in time to a voyage or a short period and the unexpired terms of these risks if war began would of course be shorter still. An early reduction of liability would be possible. In life assurance we are dealing with a permanent contract and the chance of a catastrophic loss in war is far less.* There are, however, cases in which a prudent insurer might exclude war risk because an unduly large loss might occur. One of them would be if a large number of employees in a single building or block of buildings were insured under a group insurance scheme not associated with a pension scheme arranged with the same insurer. Group insurance is a one-year risk and the insurer would have as a reserve little more than the proportion of premiums appropriate to the unexpired term. The loss to the insurer is therefore the full sum assured on each life and not, as in the case of permanent life assurance, the sum assured less substantial reserves ascertained in accordance with the usual kind of actuarial valuation. The war risk in such a group insurance would be increased if the position of the building or the nature of the work were such as to render the building a likely object for attack. A somewhat similar problem may arise in connection with insuring employers against liability to pay compensation or damages to workmen in their employment. This liability would be greatly increased in any case in which the Courts

* I dealt with this problem in a lecture given in Munich in July 1937, explaining that the difficulties in war lay, not only in increased mortality, but rather in losses from taxation, defaults in interest payments, depreciation of assets and, so far as the assured are concerned, in currency depreciation.

should hold that the injuries sustained during aerial or naval bombardment arose "out of and in the course of" employment.

I merely mention these risks to remind you that there are many ways in which war may affect insurers, but it is the definite insurance of property against the risks of war with which we are dealing and we must not confuse the issue by allowing our thoughts to wander outside our real province.

It has been suggested that a sort of insurance against, or a compensation for damage done in war, could be arranged in a different way and a company has been formed with this in view. This is what may be called a mutual pooling scheme. The idea is to collect a premium, or perhaps it would be better to say a contribution, at a certain rate admitting that it may be inadequate, to put aside the contributions, and, if there is a war, to use the sum available towards the damage suffered by contributors, while, if there should not be a war, the fund available would be distributed after an agreed number of years. This sort of concern differs from an existing insurance company in that it is set up for the particular purpose: it has no reserve outside the contributions, less expenses, and it does not use an existing organisation to obtain business. But the inherent weakness is, I think, the same: the real risk of loss is unknown and even if a substantial sum is invested depreciation of assets will materially reduce it.

We will now consider the possibility of a Government insurance scheme. It may seem that in some respects the Government would be in a better position to grant war risk insurance than insurance companies and underwriters, because Governments should be better informed as to the probable extent of damage in the event of war and better judges of the chance of a war. This should be the case and, probably, the Government is in possession of information not available elsewhere, but I am sure no responsible Government official would admit that the Government can make an approximate estimate of the cost of war risks nor could he measure accurately the chance of war. In fact on 4th May, 1937, the then President of the Board of Trade (Mr Runciman) stated that, after a careful review of all the circumstances, the Government had reached the conclusion that no scheme of insurance of property in this country against war risks on land would be appropriate to the conditions of a future war so far as they could be foreseen.

Let us, however, try to evolve some sort of scheme bearing in mind the difficulties we have already discussed. We must avoid a selection against the Government so as to prevent a state of affairs when all the London dock property is insured but isolated houses in Westmorland or the Dales are uninsured. In other words we will imagine a national scheme. Further, as the loss is really a national one, it seems reasonable to spread the risk over all property and make a level rate of assessment—this has the further advantage of simplicity. Let us assume that a Government makes the scheme compulsory and premiums are collected. This means, in effect, that the Government undertakes to replace all the damage from hostile aircraft and bombardment and makes an annual levy against the possible loss. If there is no war in the first year what will the Government do with the levy? A possible course would be to use it in reduction of debt on the ground that such a course would give a little more margin for borrowing to meet subsequent war risk liabilities, but if there were a war in the first year then, clearly, the Government should see to the replacement of damaged property or pay equivalent compensation. Now this is well nigh impossible.

In the throes of war, no Government could take men off armament or essential war work to replace damage, whereas, if it issued Government bonds to the estimated value of the damage the recipients in the early days of the war would have far less than the original payment, owing to depreciation, compared with recipients at the end of the war. A payment during the war in terms of money or bonds would be meaningless because money values change so rapidly during a war, and the cost of replacement after the war might have no reasonable relation to the payments made in war time. In other words, even a Government would be hard put to it to produce a scheme. It may be said that during the last war air risk insurance was granted under a Government scheme, but to some extent, as already explained, it is safer to grant such insurance when a war is present than when the unknown chance of a war occurring has to be taken into account. Even if insurance may have been possible in 1915, have we any justification for saying that in altered conditions it would be equally possible? A Government might, in the future, repeat the experiment of such a scheme and take responsibility for replacement or compensation in respect of damage only when a property was insured under its scheme. I do not think this can be considered fully satisfactory, and a comprehensive responsibility seems appropriate to a national emergency. It might, however, be possible to achieve the result using, as before, existing insurers as intermediaries, and a scheme devised with the intention of making it as nearly comprehensive as possible could be brought into force immediately a war started by a new "Defence of the Realm Act".

Another suggestion has been made, namely that the Government should start a scheme now and use the premiums or contributions towards its defence schemes on the ground that this is an attempt by a Government to insure its nationals against the risks of war. This seems to me merely to bring us to the wider problem of the best way of meeting the cost of armament: the Government has already instituted a National Defence Contribution and, however little we may like its present form, an extension so that the Government collected contributions from all owners of property of any kind would lead merely to another form of general taxation.

Is there then no solution to the problem and must property owners face the unhappy position that if they lose anything in an air raid or bombardment compensation is impossible? I do not consider that is the correct inference. When war comes the Government might then put into operation some scheme such as that used in the last war or, alternatively, when the war is over it could then replace or compensate. A record of losses would have to be made (possibly with the help of existing insurers), and the cost of replacement could be estimated and spread fairly over the community as a whole. Perhaps arrangements on some such lines as this are what the Government intends, but it seems clear from Government statements that there is no intention of attempting to provide a Government insurance scheme in advance—and that decision seems to me entirely reasonable.

It is easy for an insurance man to say "The public wants insurance against war risk—let us give it to them". But what we should give them is not really insurance: I do not believe in deluding the public by a pretence, and I feel sure that a careful review of the position will carry the conviction that insurance against war risks at the present time is an impossibility.